STORYLAND

1

Student's Book

Lisiane Ott Schulz

Luciana Santos Pinheiro

Storyland Student's Site Access Code:
Storyland1@students

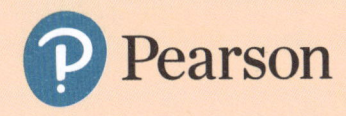

Pearson

Head of Product - Pearson Brasil	Juliano Costa
Product Manager - Pearson Brasil	Marjorie Robles
Product Coordinator - ELT	Mônica Bicalho
Authors	Lisiane Ott Schulz
	Luciana Santos Pinheiro
Collaborators	Fernanda Bressan Capelini
	Indiana Oliveira
	Milena Schneid Eich
	Sofia Xanthopoulos Bordin
	Verônica Bombassaro
Editor - ELT	Simara H. Dal'Alba
Editorial Assistant - ELT	Sandra Vergani Dall'Agnol
Proofreader	Silva Serviços de Educação
Proofreader (Portuguese):	Fernanda R. Braga Simon
Copyeditor	Maria Estela Alcântara
Teacher's Guide (Portuguese translation)	Eduardo Lubisco Portella
Pedagogical Reviewer	Márcia Marques Goulart
Quality Control	Renata S. C. Victor
Product Design Coordinator	Rafael Lino
Art Editor - ELT	Emily Andrade
Production Editors	Daniel Reis
	Vitor Martins
Acquisitions and permissions Manager	Maiti Salla
Acquisitions and permissions	Sandra Sebastião
Graphic design	Mirella Della Maggiore Armentano
	APIS design integrado
Graphic design (cover)	Daniel Reis
	Emily Andrade
	Mirella Della Maggiore Armentano
Illustration (cover)	Leandro Marcondes
Illustrated by	Alex Cói	Estúdio Secreto
	Dayane Cabral
	Leandro Marcondes
	Víctor Lemos
Content Development	Allya Language Solutions
Media Development	Estação Gráfica
Audio	Maximal Studio

Every effort has been made to trace the copyright holders and we apologize in advance for any unintentional omissions. We would be pleased to insert the appropriate acknowledgement in any subsequent edition of this publication.

Dados Internacionais de Catalogação na Publicação (CIP)
(Câmara Brasileira do Livro, SP, Brasil)

Schulz, Lisiane Ott
  Storyland 1: Student's Book / Lisiane Ott Schulz, Luciana Santos Pinheiro ; [coordenação Monica Bicalho]. -- 1. ed. -- São Paulo : Pearson Education do Brasil, 2018.

Vários ilustradores.
ISBN 978-85-430-2623-7

1. Inglês (Educação infantil) I. Pinheiro, Luciana Santos. II. Bicalho, Monica. III. Título.

18-17166   CDD-372.21

Índices para catálogo sistemático:
1. Inglês : Educação infantil 372.21
Maria Alice Ferreira - Bibliotecária - CRB-8/7964

ISBN 978-85-430-2623-7 (Student's Book)

STORYLAND

Student's Book 1

UNIT 1	The Ugly Duckling	8
UNIT 2	The Gingerbread Man	16
UNIT 3	The Tale Of Peter Rabbit	24
UNIT 4	The Boy Who Cried Wolf	32
UNIT 5	The Frog Prince	40
UNIT 6	This Little Piggy	48
UNIT 7	The Standing Tin Soldier	56
UNIT 8	The North Wind And The Sun	64

Press-outs 73

Stickers 89

Scope and Sequence

UNIT	THEME	VALUES	OBJECTIVES	MAIN LANGUAGE	SONG	CLIL
1 The Ugly Duckling	Numbers and Colors	Respect differences and be friends	• Understand and name the colors *blue* and *yellow* • Count to five	blue, yellow; one, two, three, four, five; duck, egg, nest, swan	Five little ducks	Art: Make a sensory bag
2 The Gingerbread Man	My Face and Shapes	Learn to be persistent and keep trying	• Identify and name parts of the face • Identify and name shapes	ears, eyes, face, nose, mouth; circle, square, triangle; green, orange, red; What color is this? What color are these?	Humpty Dumpty	Art: Make a funny face collage
3 The Tale Of Peter Rabbit	My Family	Follow parents' instructions; Eat just enough (not too much or too little)	• Identify and name family members • Answer questions beginning with *who* and *where*	mommy, daddy, baby, brother, sister, rabbit; Who is this? Where is Daddy? Is this Mommy?	The finger family	Social Science: Make a table mat
4 The Boy Who Cried Wolf	Night and Day	Tell the truth; Take good care of animals	• Identify the feelings *happy* and *sad* • Understand the difference between *night* and *day*	evening, morning, night; moon, star, sun; boy, girl, man, woman; happy, sad; Is he happy?	Twinkle, twinkle little star	Art: Make your own Starry Night

UNIT	THEME	VALUES	OBJECTIVES	MAIN LANGUAGE	SONG	CLIL
5 The Frog Prince	Our Nature	Be kind to people and make friends	• Identify and name elements in a garden • Count to six	flowers, garden, grass, tree; frog, ladybug; one, two, three, four, five, six; How many?	Ladybug	Art & Math: Make a ladybug
6 This Little Piggy	Food and Fruits	Cheer up friends	• Identify and name fruits and other kinds of food	apple, banana, grape, orange, pear; pancake, roast beef, salad; Do you like pancakes?	Mix a pancake	Cooking: Make a fruit salad
7 The Standing Tin Soldier	Toys and Musical Instruments	Share and take care of personal belongings	• Identify and name toys • Identify and name musical instruments	doll, ballerina; castle, car, paper boat, soldier; bells, drums, flute, trombone; Let's play the drums.	The finger band	Music, art, & craft: Make a drum
8 The North Wind And The Sun	Weather	Understand that everyone is unique	• Distinguish between *hot* and *cold* • Identify weather conditions: *rain*, *sun*, and *wind*	rain, sun, wind; hot, cold; coat; spider; down, up	Itsy-bitsy spider	Science and Drama: Act out a rain storm

We are in Storyland!

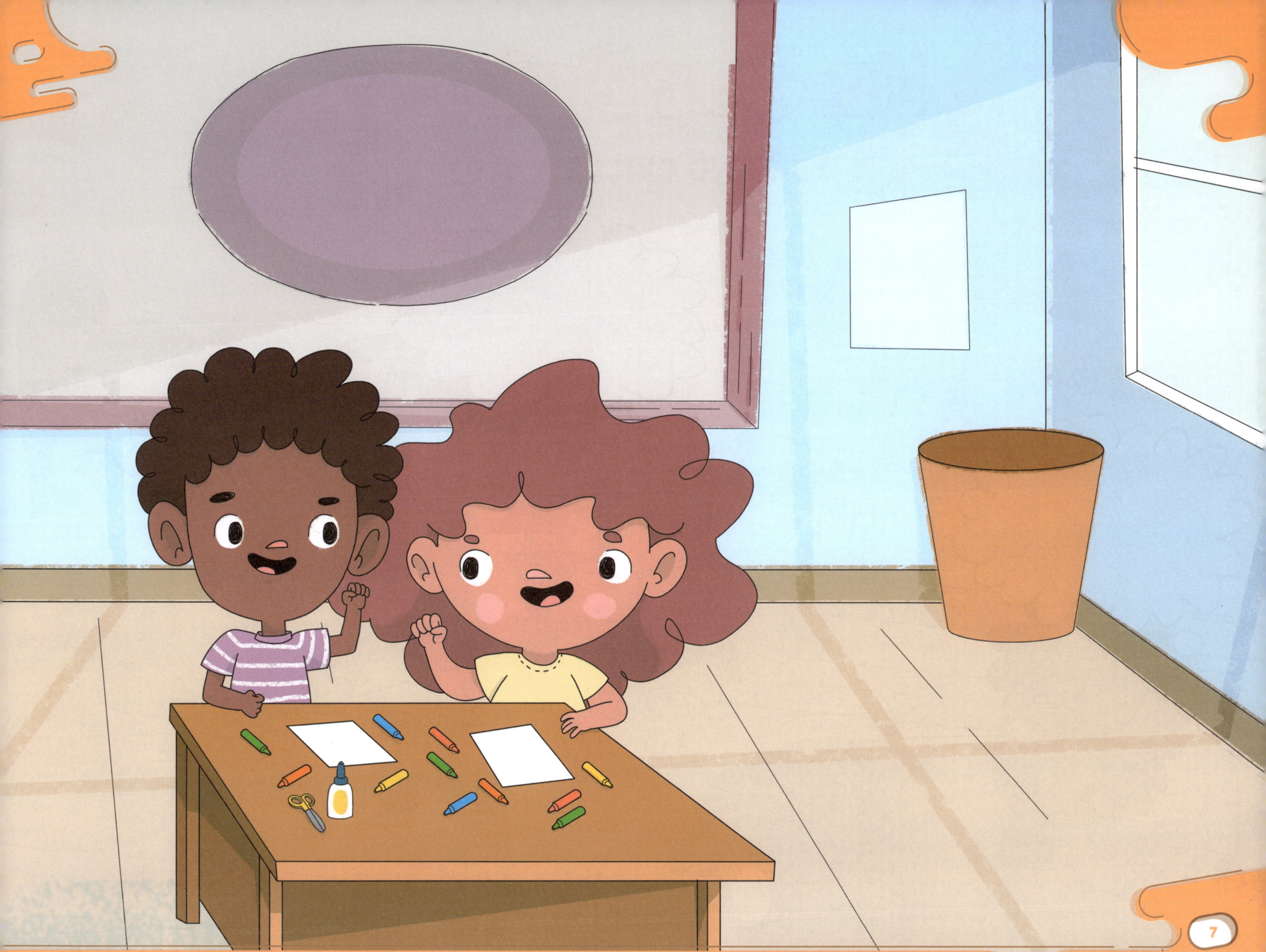

The Ugly Duckling

1 LOOK AND CIRCLE.

2 LISTEN AND STICK.

TRACK 04

LESSON 1

STORY

3 LISTEN AND REPEAT. THEN COLOR.

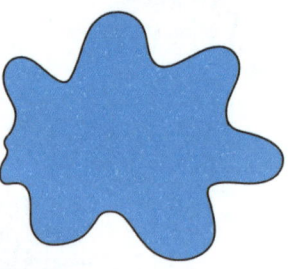

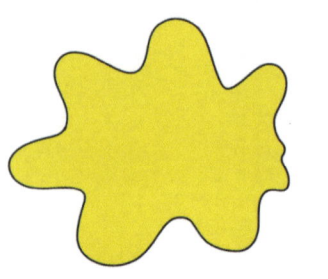

TRACK 05

LESSON 2

4 LOOK, COUNT, AND TRACE.

LESSON 2

5 LOOK, LISTEN, AND SING.

TRACK 06

LESSON 3

6 LISTEN AND GLUE. TRACK 31

LESSON 3

1	2	3
4	5	6

7 TRACE.

SING

LESSON 4

8 SORT OUT AND COUNT.

MATH CLIL — LESSON 4

UNIT 2 THE GINGERBREAD MAN

LESSON 1

1 LOOK AND CIRCLE.

2 LISTEN, TRACE, AND COLOR.

TRACK 07

LESSON 1

STORY

3 TRACE A LINE.

LESSON 2

4 LISTEN, REPEAT, AND STICK.

TRACK 08

LESSON 2

5 LISTEN AND SING. THEN CIRCLE.

LESSON 3

6 GLUE.

LESSON 3

1	2	3
4	5	6

7 LISTEN, POINT, AND REPEAT. TRACK 10

LESSON 4

8 MAKE A FUNNY FACE COLLAGE.

ART + CLIL

LESSON 4

23

UNIT 3: The Tale Of Peter Rabbit

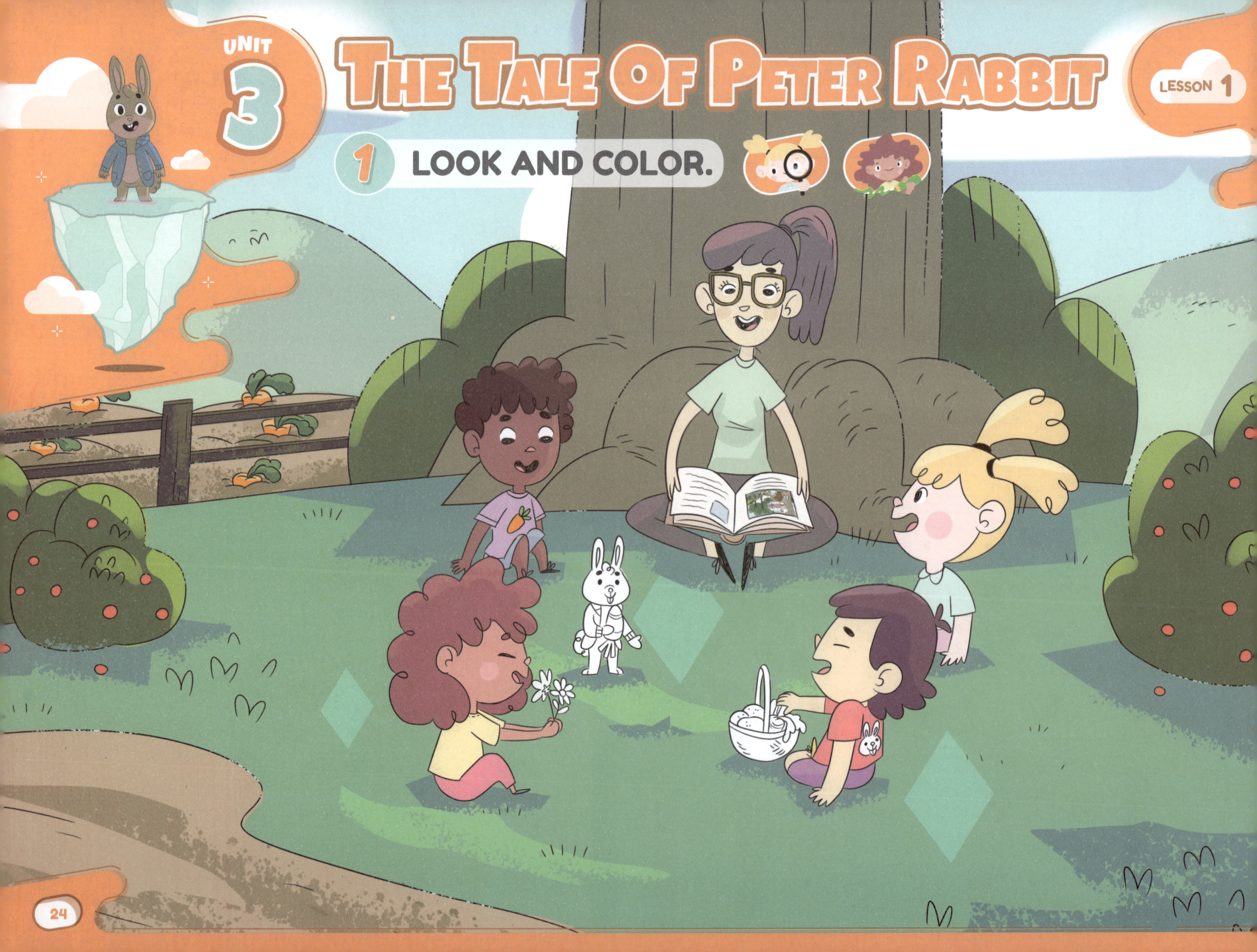

LESSON 1

1 LOOK AND COLOR.

2 LISTEN AND STICK. TRACK 11

LESSON 1

STORY

3 LISTEN, POINT, AND REPEAT. THEN MATCH.

TRACK 12

LESSON 2

4 LOOK, TRACE, AND COLOR.

Lesson 2

5 LOOK, LISTEN, AND SING.

TRACK 13

LESSON 3

SING

6 LISTEN AND GLUE.

TRACK 14

LESSON 3

1	2	3
4	5	6

7 MATCH.

8 MAKE A FAMILY TABLE MAT.

SOCIAL SCIENCE CLIL — LESSON 4

UNIT 4 — The Boy Who Cried Wolf

LESSON 1

1 LOOK AND CIRCLE.

2 LISTEN AND STICK.

TRACK 15

LESSON 1

STORY

3 LISTEN AND MATCH.

TRACK 16

Lesson 2

DAY

NIGHT

4 CUT, PLAY, AND GLUE.

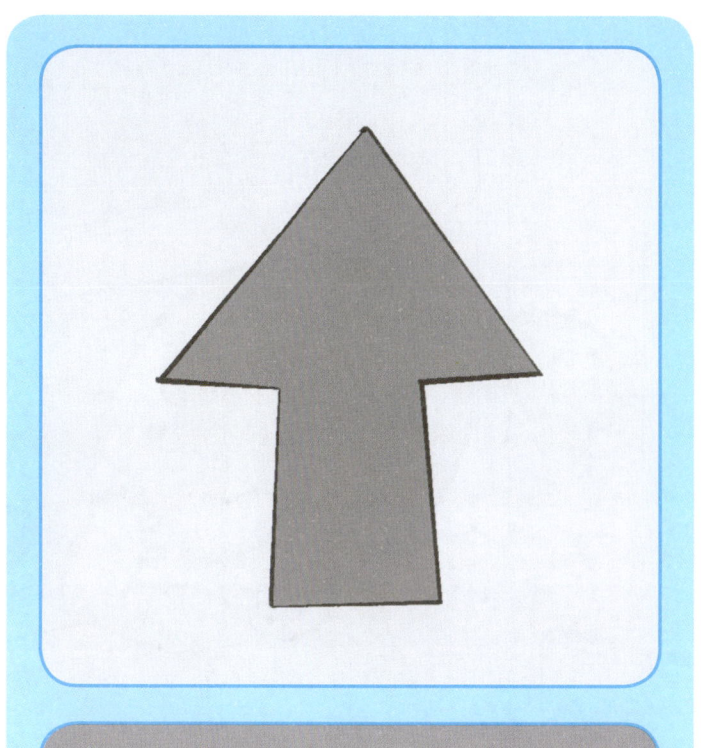

LESSON 2

5 LISTEN AND SING. THEN COLOR. TRACK 17 LESSON 3

6 LOOK AND COLOR.

LESSON 3

7 CIRCLE.

Lesson 4

8 MAKE YOUR OWN STARRY NIGHT.

ART CLIL — LESSON 4

UNIT 5: The Frog Prince

LESSON 1

1 LOOK AND COLOR.

2 LISTEN AND STICK.

TRACK 18

LESSON 1

STORY

3 COUNT AND MATCH.

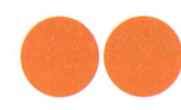

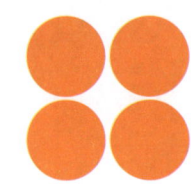

4 COLOR AND COUNT.

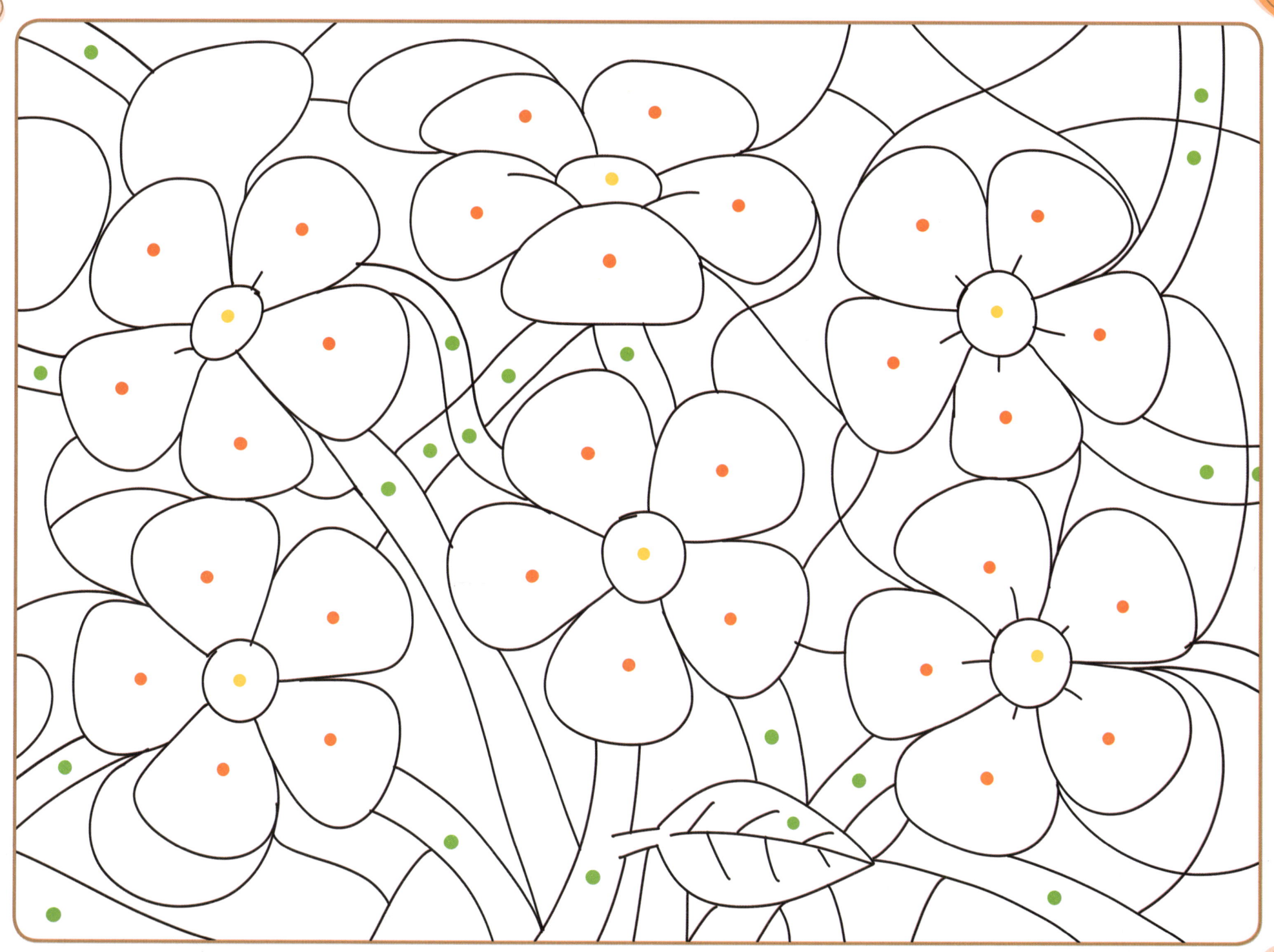

LESSON 2

5 LISTEN AND SING. THEN CIRCLE.

TRACK 19

LESSON 3

6 LISTEN AND GLUE.

LESSON 3

7 LOOK AND TRACE.

Lesson 4

8 MAKE A LADYBUG.

ART & MATH — CLIL

LESSON 4

47

UNIT 6 — This Little Piggy

LESSON 1

1 FIND AND CIRCLE.

2 LISTEN AND STICK.

TRACK 21

LESSON 1

STORY

49

3 LISTEN AND MATCH.

TRACK 22

LESSON 2

4 CUT AND GLUE.

LESSON 2

5 LISTEN AND SING. FIND AND CIRCLE.

TRACK 23

LESSON 3

6 LISTEN AND GLUE.

TRACK 24

LESSON 3

7 LOOK, COUNT, AND CIRCLE.

LESSON 4

8 MAKE A FRUIT SALAD.

COOKING CLIL

LESSON 4

UNIT 7 The Standing Tin Soldier

LESSON 1

1 LOOK AND CHECK.

2 LISTEN AND STICK.

TRACK 25

LESSON 1

STORY

57

3 FIND AND CIRCLE.

LESSON 2

4 MATCH. THEN COLOR.

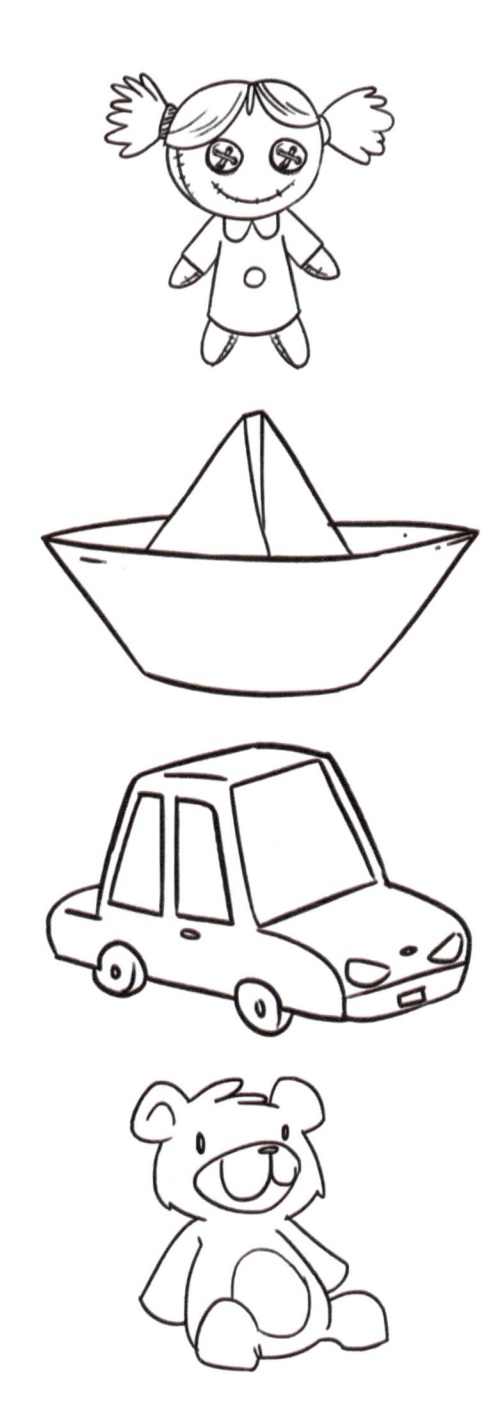

LESSON 2

5 LISTEN AND CIRCLE.

TRACK 26

SING

LESSON 3

6 GLUE.

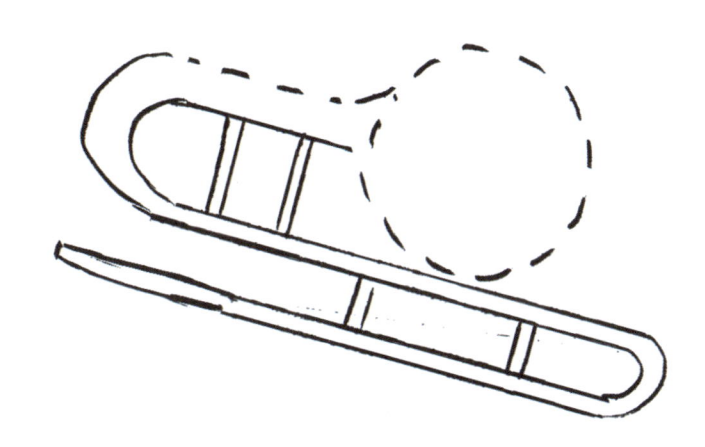

LESSON 3

7. LISTEN AND GLUE.

TRACK 27

LESSON 4

1	2	3
4	5	6

8 MAKE A DRUM.

MUSIC, ART & CRAFTS — CLIL

LESSON 4

UNIT 8
The North Wind And The Sun

1 LOOK AND CIRCLE.

2 LISTEN AND STICK.

TRACK 28

LESSON 1

STORY

3 LOOK AND CIRCLE.

LESSON 2

4 GLUE.

LESSON 2

5 POINT, LISTEN, AND SING.

TRACK 25

LESSON 3

6 ACT OUT AND SING. TRACK 30

LESSON 3

SING

7 LOOK AND DRAW.

LESSON 4

8 ACT OUT A RAIN STORM.

DRAMA + CLIL LESSON 4

Press-outs & Stickers

Press-outs

UNIT 1

Press-outs

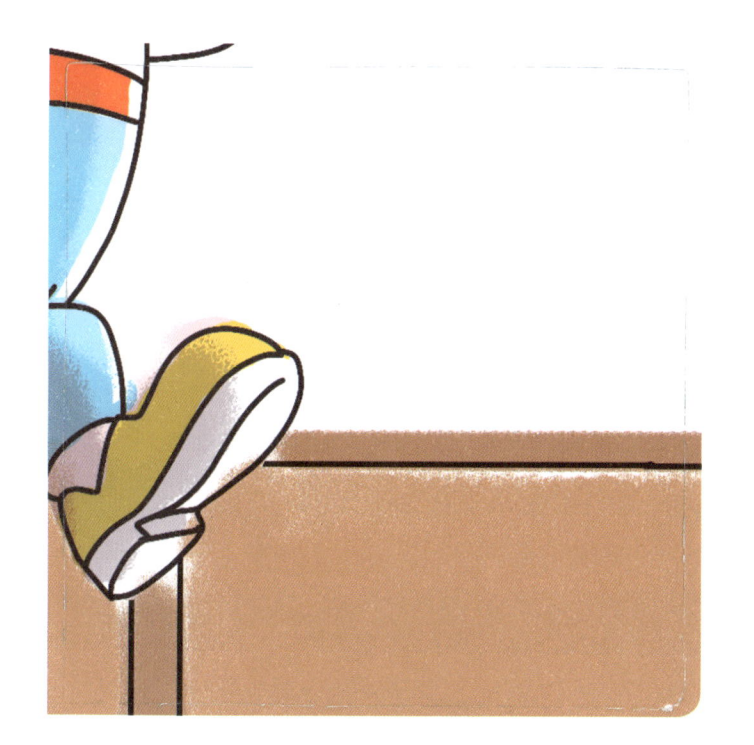

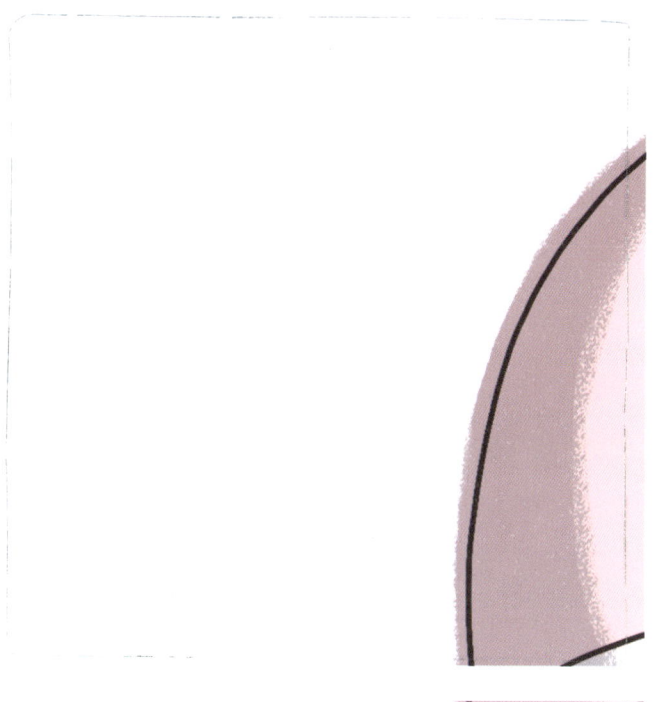

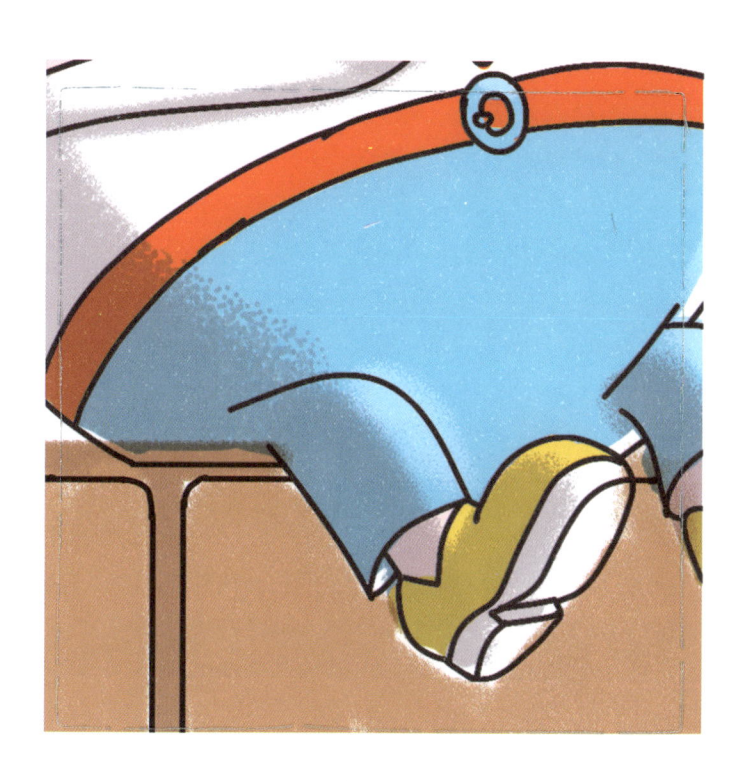

UNIT 2

Press-outs

UNIT 3

Press-outs

UNIT 4

Press-outs

UNIT 5

Press-outs

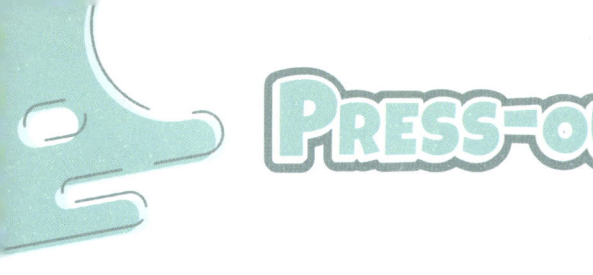

UNIT 6

Press-outs

UNIT 7

Press-outs

UNIT 8

AND STORYLAND STORYLAND STORYLAND STORYLAND STORYLAND STORYLAND S
ORYLAND STORYLAND STORYLAND STORYLAND STORYLAND STORYLAND STORYL
AND STORYLAND STORYLAND STORYLAND STORYLAND STORYLAND STORYLAND S
ORYLAND STORYLAND STORYLAND STORYLAND STORYLAND STORYLAND STORYL
AND STORYLAND STORYLAND STORYLAND STORYLAND STORYLAND STORYLAND S
ORYLAND STORYLAND STORYLAND STORYLAND STORYLAND STORYLAND STORYL
AND STORYLAND STORYLAND STORYLAND STORYLAND STORYLAND STORYLAND S
ORYLAND STORYLAND STORYLAND STORYLAND STORYLAND STORYLAND STORYL
AND STORYLAND STORYLAND STORYLAND STORYLAND STORYLAND STORYLAND S
ORYLAND STORYLAND STORYLAND STORYLAND STORYLAND STORYLAND STORYL
AND STORYLAND STORYLAND STORYLAND STORYLAND STORYLAND STORYLAND S
ORYLAND STORYLAND STORYLAND STORYLAND STORYLAND STORYLAND STORYL
AND STORYLAND STORYLAND STORYLAND STORYLAND STORYLAND STORYLAND S
ORYLAND STORYLAND STORYLAND STORYLAND STORYLAND STORYLAND STORYL
AND STORYLAND STORYLAND STORYLAND STORYLAND STORYLAND STORYLAND S
ORYLAND STORYLAND STORYLAND STORYLAND STORYLAND STORYLAND STORYL
AND STORYLAND STORYLAND STORYLAND STORYLAND STORYLAND STORYLAND S
ORYLAND STORYLAND STORYLAND STORYLAND STORYLAND STORYLAND STORYL

Stickers

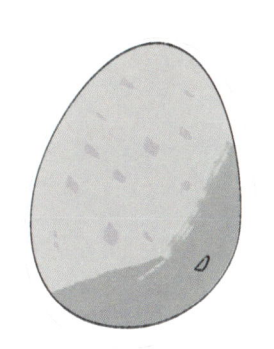

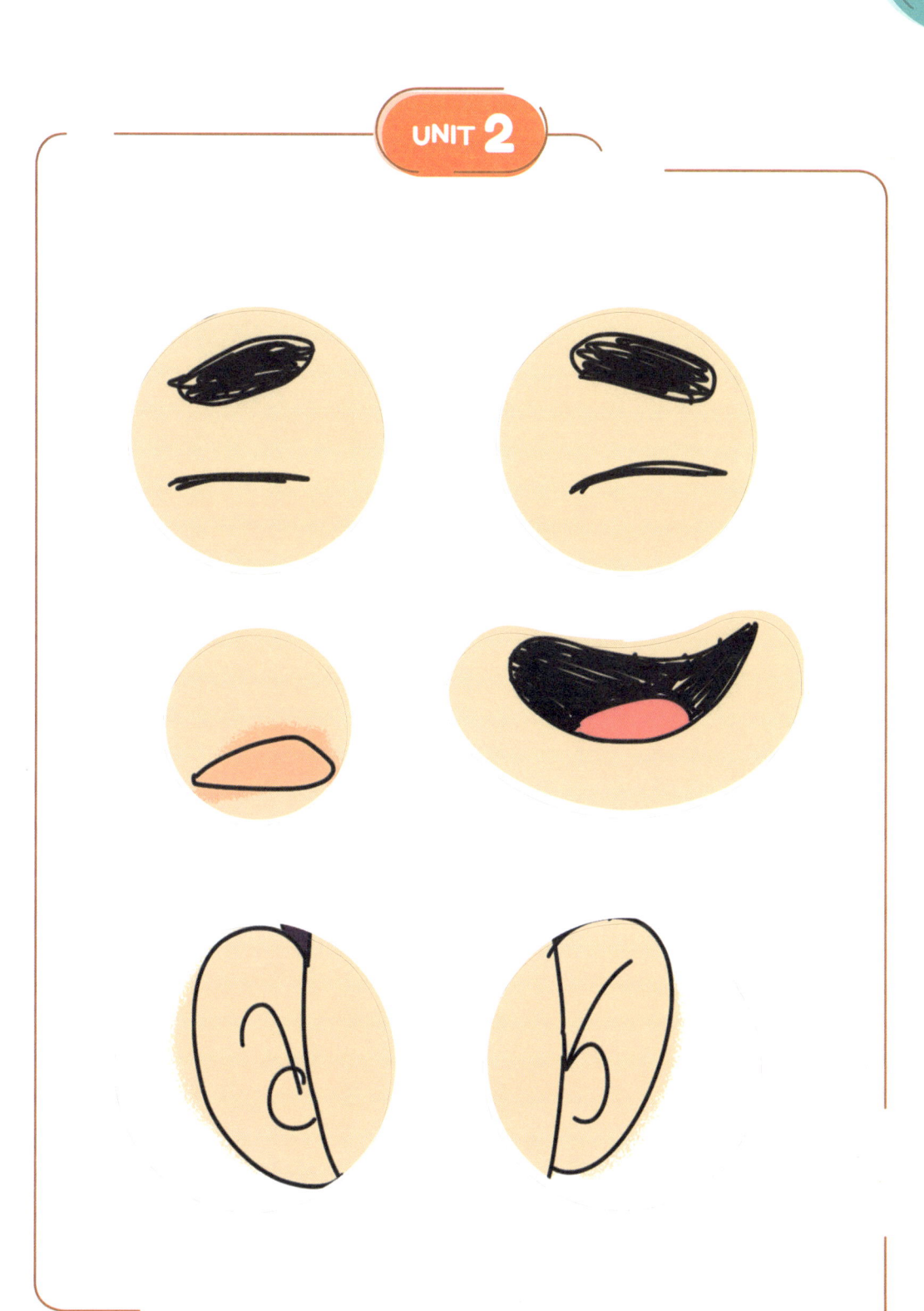

UNIT 1

UNIT 2

Stickers

UNIT 3

UNIT 4

Stickers

UNIT **5**

UNIT **6**

Stickers

UNIT 7

UNIT 8

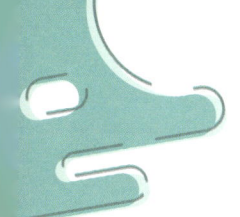

Cover Stickers